JAPAN
AND THE
UNITED STATES
Economic Competitors

Mary Ellen Snodgrass

THE MILLBROOK PRESS
Brookfield, Connecticut

Published by The Millbrook Press
2 Old New Milford Road
Brookfield, CT 06804
© 1993 Blackbirch Graphics, Inc.
First Edition
5 4 3 2 1

Created and produced in association with Blackbirch Graphics.
Series Editor: Bruce S. Glassman

Library of Congress Cataloging-in-Publication Data
Snodgrass, Mary Ellen.
  Japan and the United States: economic competitors/by Mary Ellen Snodgrass.
        p.   cm. — (Headliners)
  Includes bibliographical references and index.
  Summary: Examines the cultural and historical roots of the economic rivalry between the United States and Japan and discusses options for the future.
    1. United States—Foreign economic relations—Japan—Juvenile literature. 2. Japan—Foreign economic relations—United States—Juvenile literature. 3. Japan—Economic conditions—1945—Juvenile literature. [1. United States—Foreign economic relations—Japan. 2. Japan—Foreign economic relations—United States.] I. Title. II. Series.
  ISBN 1-56294-374-X
  HF 1456.5.J3S66 1993
  337.52073—dc20   92-33017
                                                                 CIP
                                                                 AC

Contents

4

Chapter 1

Looking Across the Pacific

Think about the last time you went shopping for a CD player, a television set, or a portable tape player. If you made some price and quality comparisons, you most likely wound up considering a number of Japanese products as well as a few with American-sounding names, though chances are many of these were assembled in Japan or contained Japanese parts.

When it came down to finally making your choice, you probably bought a Japanese product. If you were like most Americans—or even most electronics consumers around the world—you realized that, overall, you would get better quality at a lower price if you bought Japanese.

If buying Japanese bothered you at all—perhaps because you knew that American workers were being laid off or because you wanted to help support the U.S. economy by buying American—then you shared the feelings that most Americans had toward the Japanese as we moved into the 1990s. Your American pride caused you to resent Japan somewhat, but your pocketbook directed your final move. At the cash register, without wanting to admit it, you might have even felt thankful toward the country that was able to offer such a good product at an affordable price.

The relationship between America and Japan has changed dramatically in the last fifty years.

Opposite:
A young consumer shops for a fax machine at an electronics store.

Consumers experience similar mixed emotions when shopping for other appliances, computers, and, of course, cars. These emotions reflect America's love-hate relationship with Japan. Mutual animosity and intense competition characterize this relationship. But there is also a deeper reality: The two countries need each other.

A Changing Relationship

The mixed emotions that the United States has about Japan developed from a relationship between the two countries that has changed dramatically over the past fifty years. With the bombing of Pearl Harbor in 1941, Japan became America's primary enemy. Never before had any country so deeply invaded American soil and done such extensive damage.

After World War II ended, America became an economic mentor for the devastated and humbled Japanese. In an effort to rebuild the great damage it had caused (partly by dropping atomic bombs on the cities of Hiroshima and Nagasaki), the United States spent immense resources on bringing technology and other aid to Japan.

The Japanese—who suffered a great inferiority complex from their defeat in the war—submitted to the Americans, eagerly soaking up every bit of help and advice they could get from the world's greatest free market. America enjoyed playing the role of "big brother," relishing its power and standing as a leader and teacher to the world. As Columbia University historian Carol Gluck said in a 1992 *Time* magazine article, "The Japanese depended on depending on the Americans, and the Americans depended on being depended upon."

By the late 1980s and early 1990s, however, the tide had turned completely. Now America was suffering from the inferiority complex, and Japan had assumed the role of economic mentor to the world. Americans were not used to feeling economically vulnerable. What's more, they were confused by, and resentful of, the fact that their own "students" were now surpassing them in economic success and prosperity.

The nation of Japan commanded a dynamic and powerful economy—the second largest in the world. Some economic analysts projected that, by the end of the century, Japan would overtake the United States and have the largest and most influential economy in the world. This projection came at a time when the outlook for the United States was grim. America's economy, stalled after many months of recession, needed a complete overhaul to adjust to the new world order. Communism was dead, the economic power of the European Community was growing quickly, and competition from the Japanese was pressuring American management and labor to improve product quality while reducing costs.

The economic strains that the United States was feeling in the early 1990s caused Americans to target their anger and frustration toward the prosperous Japanese. Not only were Americans squirming at the prospect of losing their economic standing in the world, but they resented their growing reliance on Japanese investment, trade, and goods.

For American business and industry, however, Japanese wealth was a double-edged sword. Japanese investment helped to keep the economy alive, but their increasing influence and control in America was troublesome. What most Americans really wanted was to deny the Japanese access to American businesses, but again their pocketbooks dictated otherwise.

The Japanese View of America

Just as Americans had conflicting feelings toward the Japanese, so, too, did the Japanese have mixed emotions about Americans. On one hand, many Japanese still felt indebted to the United States for its help after the war. As

American culture is extremely popular in Japan and is often imitated as the "hippest" in the world.

Prime Minister Kiichi Miyazawa said in a January 1992 speech, "It is no exaggeration to say that Japan could not have achieved its postwar prosperity had it not been for the good-hearted support of the U.S." On the other hand, the strong Japanese values of hard work and success have caused many Japanese to be repulsed by what they see as America's tendency toward self-indulgence, lax morals, and a lack of efficiency and discipline.

While many Japanese watched their country quickly becoming the most powerful economy in the world, they also acknowledged that they couldn't succeed alone. Japan still relied on America to export goods that are simply not available on the island. Moreover, while many Japanese looked down on American society as a sloppy mess of races and cultures that are constantly tugging the country in opposite directions, they avidly admired and imitated America. Equaling or surpassing America had become the sole standard for measuring national success. In daily life, products of American culture were among the biggest sellers in Japan, and they set music, entertainment, fashion, and life-style trends.

In the chapters that follow, we will explore in detail the history of the relationship between these two great nations. We will examine the various economic and social factors that shaped this relationship in the 1990s, and we will see that, for every negative that exists between Japan and America, there seems to be a positive as well. Most of all, it will become clear that, despite their differences, conflicts, and intense competition, these two nations depend on each other for their very survival.

Chapter 2

An Island Nation Evolves

Japan, known to its people as Nippon, which means source of the rising sun, is a small nation made up of over three thousand volcanic islands bounded by the Pacific Ocean, the China Sea, and the Sea of Japan. With a land mass of 145,870 square miles, it is slightly smaller than the state of Montana and has over 5,857 miles of coastline. In terms of people and available land, Japan ranked eighth in the world in population per square mile during the 1990s. At that time, almost 77 percent of its population was urban, and an average of 853 citizens were packed into each square mile.

Japan's major cities include Tokyo, the capital, which is home to over 8 million of the nation's 124 million people; Yokohama, which houses over 3 million Japanese; and Osaka with over two-and-a-half million people.

Currently governed by a constitutional monarchy, Japan was once an isolated empire dating to the fourth century B.C. During the Middle Ages, it evolved a warrior culture based on a military elite known as the *samurai*. This concentrated power helped the nation to shape a culture related to, but separate from, China, a country it had long copied.

For centuries, Japan was a trader nation dependent on its own supplies of fish, rice, and tea. It produced silks,

> Japan is smaller than the state of Montana, but ranks eighth in world population per square mile.

Opposite:
A block in one of Japan's busiest commercial districts, downtown Tokyo.

pottery, enamelware, and pearls to exchange for goods (particularly firearms) from Chinese and Western markets. As Japan's military leaders tightened their control on the country, they tried to stop all Western influence, especially Christianity, which threatened the practice of Buddhism, Japan's major religion. The nation also remained virtually racially pure, a boast that brought pride to leaders who demanded that outsiders be kept away. At the beginning of the nineteenth century, Japan also attempted to isolate itself from a prosperous world economy that grew rich after the invention of the clipper ship, which sped trade goods around the globe and increased contact between richly diverse cultures. In 1853, Commodore Matthew C. Perry, an American naval commander, forced his way into Japan and, within four years, opened its markets to outside influences.

Becoming a World Power

As a budding power in world trade in the 1800s, Japan, which bases its monetary system on the yen, actively courted U.S. and European markets. Outside influences also raised Japan's standard of living and its awareness of modern methods of medicine, warfare, education, travel and communications, and other forms of technology (especially printing). Inspired by Emperor Meiju, Japan's great modernizer, citizens copied U.S. and European competitors by opening their own businesses and factories. As Japan grew more wealthy and powerful in the late 1800s and early 1900s, its leaders sought to expand the nation's influence over Korea, Russia, and China, which had grown weaker and less prosperous during those same years. Japanese armies defeated China in 1895 and Russia in 1905 and colonized parts of Korea and Manchuria soon after.

During the early 1930s, the Great Depression gripped economies all over the world. Like most major industrial nations, Japan began to founder economically. By 1940, Japan was pursuing an agenda of aggressive expansionism, looking to strengthen its political ties as well as improve its economy. In an effort to align itself with stronger nations, Japan allied itself with Germany and Italy, two nations that had already been aggressively fighting a war of domination in Europe. Together, Germany, Italy, and Japan were referred to as the Axis powers.

Once Japan joined with these other two nations, the United States severed all trade ties with the country and instituted embargoes—laws forbidding trade—on oil and scrap iron. The embargoes hurt Japan's weakening economy and created even stronger anti-American sentiment in the island nation. On December 7, 1941, Japan's animosity toward America fueled its decision to carry out a first strike on U.S. military installations in Hawaii. By bombing Pearl Harbor in a surprise attack, the Japanese

On December 7, 1941, Japan bombed U.S. military installations at Pearl Harbor, Hawaii.

hoped to gain the upper hand in the Pacific and go on to victory with the Axis powers. Instead, the attack propelled the United States into the war with a motivated military determined to fight the "yellow peril" of Japanese aggression. On December 8, 1941, America declared war on Japan and its allies.

Encouraged by success at the beginning of the war, Japan's general Hideki Tojo maneuvered into the U.S. territories of Guam, the Philippines, and Midway, seriously crippling the U.S. Navy. In the United States, anti-Japanese feeling and government concerns that Japanese Americans might endanger the war effort spread across the nation. In 1942, these sentiments provoked President Roosevelt to issue Executive Order 9066, confining over 120,000 U.S. citizens of Japanese parentage to internment camps. The most infamous of these, Camp Manzanar, was built on the western edge of the Mojave Desert in dusty, dry territory. There, Japanese Americans who had previously been upstanding members of society tried to lead normal lives in spite of inadequate rations, internal unrest, and miserable, cramped quarters. Even though many of these internees were born in the United States, they were denied basic American freedoms. As a result, they were subjected to hateful prejudice as they lost their homes, personal belongings, and businesses.

During this same period—and partly in retaliation for U.S. internment camps—the Japanese army established prisoner-of-war camps in Los Baños and Santo Tomás, outside Manila in the Philippines. These primitive and brutal prisons—notorious for such things as torture, disease, and starvation—contained over seven thousand American civilians. Bill Loughlin, of the Glendale (California) *News Press* wrote at the time that, "more than four hundred civilians died in those Philippine Island camps. . . . Those who survived lost everything."

General Hideki Tojo led Japan's efforts during World War II.

In order to avoid a conventional invasion of Japan in 1945, the United States dropped atomic bombs on the Japanese cities of Hiroshima and Nagasaki. Here, a survivor surveys the destruction at Hiroshima.

On August 6, 1945, under orders from President Harry S. Truman, the U.S. military dropped the experimental atomic bomb on the Japanese city of Hiroshima. Three days later, on August 9, Nagasaki was bombed. The bombs were used, the president explained, to prevent additional American loss of life that would have resulted from a conventional invasion. By September 2, this unprecedented use of atomic weapons ended World War II in the Pacific. It left behind, however, massive destruction, death, and radiation poisoning among Japanese civilians that would affect lives for generations. U.S. and Japanese hatred only intensified with the unleashing of atomic weapons. Horror stories of innocent women and babies who were incinerated or maimed by the atomic blasts also generated intense emotions among the warring nations throughout the world.

An Occupied Nation

After the war, General Douglas MacArthur's occupation forces established an interim government in Japan. He immobilized the Japanese military, and introduced democracy. Postwar relations eased somewhat after the United States extended humanitarian aid to Japan's war-torn cities, offered reparations, and inaugurated a revitalization of Japanese industry, which had been decimated by U.S. bombing. During this period, Japanese laborers learned from Americans how to build skyscrapers and merchant ships, modernize farming techniques, and compete more fully in the world market.

American general Douglas MacArthur (left) watches as Japan's foreign minister Mamoru Shigemitsu signs the documents of surrender on September 2, 1945. Lieutenant General Richard Sutherland (center) also witnesses the signing.

Ford's Assembly Line in Japan

In 1899, Henry Ford, one of America's most creative minds, revolutionized American industry at his Detroit Automobile Company. Breaking away from earlier concepts that had factory workers each building units of a particular product, Ford mobilized his employees and sent each manufactured unit through an assembly line. Each worker provided one bit of expertise, such as chassis welding, and passed the evolving vehicle to the next worker, who might attach fenders or screw on mirrors. The vehicle continued past many hands, which bolted on doors, lowered the engine into place, upholstered seats, fitted glass to the windshield, and applied paint. To regulate the flow of units through the line required precise timing as well as a clear understanding of human factors, including worker fatigue, problem solving, and the need for interaction and feedback.

Ford's innovative and waste-reducing assembly line proved so successful that the concept was applied in various other aspects of manufacturing, such as appliances, toys, and electronics. After World War II, Japanese manufacturers, taking their cue from U.S. success stories, adapted Ford's assembly line to their factories. Within a generation, the Japanese were beating the United States at its own game. They effectively improved on the assembly line through cooperative managerial studies of worker efficiency and through the application of robotics to repetitive motions, such as stamping out templates, fastening parts together, welding, painting, and inspecting. Ironically, U.S. automakers have begun visiting Japanese plants to learn efficient assembly-line techniques from a new point of view.

Henry Ford's assembly-line concept was adapted by the Japanese after World War II.

In April 1952, the Allied occupation of Japan ended. Japan had learned much from its former enemy. During the 1950s, Japan's modernization created an economic recovery that surprised the world. By 1956, Japan took its place in the United Nations and, in 1964, became the first Asian nation to host the Olympics. By 1972, the United States had officially ended its postwar control of Japan by returning the islands it had captured during World War II, including Okinawa.

Partly as a result of World War II and the strong U.S. influence in its aftermath, Japan and America generated a new competition in the 1970s—this time in the global marketplace. During this period, however, the United States found its economic supremacy deflated by a number of serious concerns, which included a 1973 oil embargo from the Middle East's powerful oil-producing nations, or OPEC (Organization of Petroleum Exporting Countries), and the resulting worldwide energy crisis in the 1970s. A fluctuating loss or deficit in trade, loss of industrial leadership, a rise in Japanese manufacturing, increased national debt, and growing Japanese ownership of U.S. assets also became problems for the United States. All of these factors contributed to the United States slowly losing ground in its competition with Japan.

Fearful of economic chaos, the United States began to reevaluate its relationship with Japan in the 1990s, trying to reposition itself against one of its strongest economic rivals. In Japan, where more than half the nation worked in trade and manufacturing, commerce boomed. Japanese banks and insurance firms controlled sizable shares of the world's finances. Compared with the 1992 U.S. national debt of $3.5 trillion, Japan had money to spare, leading other nations with $57 billion in ready funds.

Staggering under a 1992 trade deficit that was expected to reach $80 billion in 1992, the U.S. government no longer served as Japan's financial "big brother." Now American financial and business leaders consulted the Japanese about solutions to problems of manufacturing, personnel management, finance, research, and world trade. America's huge trade deficit had completely changed the balance of power in world markets. *The Wall Street Journal* wrote that "the trade deficit symbolizes a profligate [recklessly extravagant] America, consuming more than it produces and spending more than it has. But it also represents the biggest gravy train ever for U.S. trading partners, who have been selling America all that stuff and lending the money to pay for it." Clearly, the economies of both nations had moved in very different—and seemingly opposite—directions.

Chapter 3

Different Economies

Since the 1950s, different economies have evolved in the United States and Japan. The factors that have shaped each economy are as varied as the nations themselves. In each case, however, education, technology, and societal organization have played dominant roles.

U.S. Prosperity and Military Spending

During the presidency of Dwight D. Eisenhower, the United States enjoyed unprecedented boom times. Housing and educational opportunities for veterans raised many unskilled and semiskilled laborers to the middle class. Factories sprang up to meet the demand for cars and trucks, building materials, furniture, appliances, and clothing.

Meanwhile, during the late 1940s and early 1950s, Senator Joseph McCarthy helped set off a growing paranoia based on fears that Communists were infiltrating the government, industries, the schools, and the arts and entertainment world. These fears were made more credible by the fact that the Soviet Union was known to have the atomic bomb. To guard against the "Red Menace" of Russian communism, the military required more sophisticated weapons systems and, with them,

The sharp contrast in topography between the two countries accounts for many of the differences in the economies.

Opposite:
Farmers in Wyoming harvest wheat. The U.S. economy was based for many years on agriculture, while Japan's was based on manufacturing.

greater numbers of technicians. This new demand provided ever-greater opportunities for Americans in areas ranging from high-technology factory work to upgrading highways and rail lines. Although these innovations in civil and military preparedness opened jobs, they also placed a heavy tax burden on the working class. However, because people were led to fear an attack by the USSR, they continued to favor massive military spending.

Japan's Focus on Manufacturing and Trading

In contrast to the booming military-based development in the United States during the 1950s—which fueled a deceptively healthy economy—Japan opted to grow in other directions. Because the mountainous topography of its islands provides little cultivatable land for an agricultural economy, Japan turned its focus to manufacturing and trading. It exchanged Japanese-produced goods for commodities that the country lacks—notably wheat, corn, oranges, beef, milk, butter, and cheese, all of which require extensive farmland. Japan also lacks efficient means by which to produce pharmaceuticals, airplanes, oil, and timber. Prevented by treaty regulations from raising its own army and navy for self-defense, Japan relied on American war machinery to protect its interests. As the

Between the 1950s and the 1990s, America based a large part of its economy on the production of military-related goods. The Pentagon in Washington, D.C., is the headquarters of the U.S. military.

Women in the Japanese Workplace

The two-income family is a rarity in Japan. Only 38 percent of Japan's couples work, contrasted with 58 percent in the United States. What Americans think of as "male chauvinism" may be a significant factor in the reluctance of Japanese women to enter the work force. In many areas of business, women are still commonly unrewarded, regardless of capabilities, company loyalty, or performance. As a means of cost control, according to *Forbes* magazine, company managers pride themselves on keeping female employees in clerical positions at entry-level salaries. Career opportunities for women remain basically clerical; prestige and promotions extend chiefly to males. In terms of feminism and equal rights for women, many social analysts liken Japan to America in the 1950s.

Japanese women, discouraged from choosing work over child-bearing, feel additional social and familial pressures to remain at home tending to cooking, cleaning, shopping, and child rearing. Since Japanese men are expected to devote long hours to their jobs, marriages show the strain of separation. Women are often in complete control of family finances, discipline, religion, and culture. The mother of the family, who is discouraged from producing more than two children, is generally responsible for pushing children toward successful careers, which often depend on after-school classes that concentrate on fluency in English.

American women, who sometimes pity Japanese women for their apparent lack of status and choice, might consider the matter from a somewhat different point of view. *The Economist* observes that "the United States has maintained its standard of living only because the majority of households contain two wage earners. Without those second incomes, the American standard of living would be the lowest among the major industrial nations."

United States concentrated more of its human and material resources on the military, Japan devoted its wealth to building a world-class factory system, which it developed by emulating U.S. and European models. By 1992, according to Michael Wolff's book *Where We Stand*, Japan's domestic companies achieved a net worth of $2.2 trillion, not far behind the U.S. net worth of $2.5 trillion.

Dramatically, Japan's economy began to pull ahead of competitors as world demand for quality Japanese products increased. To supply needed technicians and to offer future generations an improved standard of living, Japan developed a rigid, highly competitive education system that was supported in part by government funds. As it did with its industry, Japan based its university system and technical schools on U.S. and European models. But, as a result of the Japanese obsession with rushing to meet market needs, Japan's education system concentrated on training laborers while the U.S. educational system consistently placed greater emphasis on training managers. As a result, Japan had less managerial and top-level executives but also enjoyed a productive and reliable blue-collar work force.

The typical worker formed attitudes toward the workplace based on a strong work ethic and intense patriotism. These attitudes were encouraged by employers who offered generous benefits, including medical and dental care, credit and discounts at company stores, recreational facilities, cash incentives, and guaranteed employment. By 1992 the Japanese could boast of having one of the world's most disciplined and diligent work forces. Japanese employees were also much admired worldwide for their loyalty and longevity of service.

The United States in Second Place

As the U.S. economy developed differently from Japan's, it also began to slip in rank in the world economy. The causes for this decline were interrelated and touched upon issues of education, social welfare, national economic woes, and the basic makeup of U.S. society. While 99 percent of Japan's citizens were trained in specific skills, the U.S. educational system continued to fall short of the demands that its much larger, more complex, and much more diverse society had placed upon it. Only 76 percent of Americans graduated from high school. Partly because of its troubled educational system, many felt the United States turned out frustrated, often unmotivated people who were inadequately prepared for the workplace and less dedicated to quality products than their Japanese counterparts.

A significant obstruction to worker loyalty in the United States was also the blatant overpayment of corporate officers. According to Graeef S. Crystal in the book *In Search of Excess: The Overcompensation of American Executives:* "During the past twenty years [1970–1990], as the wages of U.S. workers fell by 13 percent, CEO

The Japanese emphasis on teamwork, cooperation, and individual responsibilities has fostered a reliable and productive work force for Japanese industry.

For decades, America neglected many of its aging mills, factories, and refineries and allowed its manufacturing facilities to decay.

(Chief Executive Officer) compensation jumped by more than 400 percent. This gap in rewards between management and labor further depletes most U.S. workers of dedication and enthusiasm for their jobs. At the same time, employers view the willingness of disgruntled workers to strike as a lack of commitment to the company."

Many believed that, in contrast to their Japanese competitors, U.S. companies had not effectively planned for their future. Ironically, America neglected many of its aging steel mills, bridges, railroads, highways, and cities during the very years that it helped to rebuild Japan. The United States also failed to recognize in time the fact that Japan was becoming a major economic threat. As a result, America allowed its own economy to founder.

Throughout the early 1990s, the United States faced many problems at home, including inner-city tensions of racial disharmony, mounting problems from unemployment and poverty, and a growing desire among women, the handicapped, and other minorities for an equal share of America's opportunities and profits. America battled issues that were all but absent from Japan's seemingly tranquil, uniform society, where women had yet to begin to respond to feminism and minorities remained mostly small, insignificant segments of the population.

Another difference that distinguished the two economies from each other was rooted in each country's concept of labor unions. In Japan, where about 26.8 percent of workers were unionized, unions encouraged a strong connection between workers and the workplace. While only 16.4 percent of the work force retains union membership in the United States, some charge that unions had spawned generations of workers who were alienated from management, productivity, and personal responsibility for quality goods. In many ways, American unions reinforced adversarial relationships between workers and employers by using strikes, sabotage, and arbitrated settlements on a regular basis. Such union practices were virtually unknown in Japan, where responsibility to group welfare attuned workers to the common good.

The future of unions, however, remains doubtful in both countries. During the 1980s, partly in response to the energy crunch and nationwide cost-cutting measures, unionism declined. In Japan, union membership declined by 13.8 percent. In the United States, where President Ronald Reagan set the tone for the decade by forcing

Between 1950 and 1990, Japan overtook the United States in world motor-vehicle production.

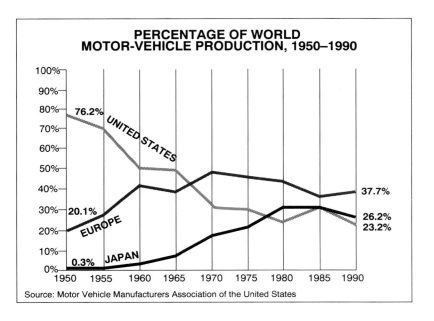

PERCENTAGE OF WORLD MOTOR-VEHICLE PRODUCTION, 1950–1990

Source: Motor Vehicle Manufacturers Association of the United States

striking air-traffic controllers to return to work or lose their jobs, membership dropped by 28.6 percent, more than twice the Japanese rate.

Also hampering the United States in the world economy was its seeming reluctance to adapt to other cultures, particularly Asian. On the whole, the United States has lacked bilingual citizens in business, neglected foreign-language programs in schools (particularly in the lower grades), and appeared to some to expect the rest of the world to speak English. Many felt another example of America's inflexibility has been its use of the outmoded English system of weights and measures, which is far more clumsy than the metric system, the system that is in general use in Japan and throughout the world.

Other American problems included a general business decline that created unemployment that hovered dangerously close to 8 percent throughout the early 1990s. Japan's unemployment rate, in contrast, was a stable 2.3 percent. This left a large number of Americans feeling discouraged. In a *USA Today* opinion poll conducted less than three months before the 1992 election, 82 percent of Americans polled doubted that politicians were capable of coping with U.S. economic problems, and 54 percent feared that the economic outlook would worsen.

Finally, in order to produce cheaper, more competitive products, U.S. businesses, since the 1980s, have increasingly moved manufacturing abroad, employing workers from Mexico, Puerto Rico, and the Philippines at low wages. This contributed to a trade imbalance in which the United States imported more foreign-made goods and exported fewer American goods. Political and governmental leaders floundered in endless debate over how to remedy this imbalance. A controversial Western Hemisphere trade pact signed by the United States, Canada, and Mexico in August 1992 was one remedy that was designed to eliminate trade barriers and promote growth through free-market competition.

"*Yoka*" vs. "Work"

Because of differences in their respective societies, workers in the United States and Japan have markedly different expectations for time that they spend outside the workplace. In Japan, this time is called *yoka,* or "time left."

In a healthy economy, most U.S. workers relish evenings, weekends, holidays, and vacations. Some employees, eager for "time off," will opt for shorter hours, early retirement, or experimental scheduling that extends the standard eight-hour workday and spreads duties over four days instead of five. A four-day workweek leaves three days for recreation, community activities, and family.

For many Japanese, such loss of work time violates a deeply ingrained work ethic; the more militant Japanese would say shorter hours and longer weekends smack of typical American laziness and irresponsibility. The Japanese work force shows its dedication to the work ethic by its attendance record: The Japanese worker misses an average of only 4.3 days per year, as contrasted with the average U.S. worker, who is absent 7.1 days. It is ironic that such diligent workers turn out so many of the world's entertainment products, like recreational vehicles, VCR's (videotape recorders), wide-screen televisions, and the karaoke, a sing-along machine.

Japan's Weaknesses

Although not so hampered by internal strife, the Japanese have been frustrated by their own weaknesses, notably a lack of originality in product design and a lack of autonomy in decision making among its workers. Because of these factors, many Japanese products tend to have a "cookie-cutter sameness."

Japanese workers have also suffered increasingly from stress. Managers shoulder tremendous workloads and spend evening hours tidying up business problems rather than relaxing with family or hobbies. Many people living in this stressful society rely heavily on tobacco and alcohol to relieve tensions resulting from severe authoritarian control, rigid long-range planning, six-day workweeks, and competition for advancement.

In Japan, promotion to the top carries with it prestige rather than monetary rewards. Japanese upper management receives smaller raises, less vacation time, and fewer privileges and titles than American upper management. In addition, because the cost of living was 40 percent higher than in the U.S. in 1992, the Japanese yen failed to buy the luxury items that the American dollar could.

Success has brought other difficulties in Japan. Because its gross national product increased by 10 percent annually from the 1950s to the 1970s, a class of young, highly paid professionals—the equivalent of U.S. "yuppies"—has emerged. This group has achieved status and prosperity quickly, partly because Japan's middle class pays only 9 percent of its salary in taxes, compared with the U.S. figure of 19 percent. As Honda CEO Takashi Matsuda remarked of this class, "For a long time there was an attitude that you had to save 20 to 30 percent of your salary. Now, young people spend everything they earn. They don't have any fear of the future."

Many Japanese have had to endure stereotyping and rejection by other cultures. Perceived in the world as crass, unsophisticated big spenders, Japanese tourists, often stereotyped by their fascination with cameras and camcorders, have borne the brunt of global ridicule. While traveling outside of Asia they have also suffered from other nations' difficulties with writing and speaking their complex language, which hamper communication with much of Western society.

One change that will seriously affect the growth of Japan's economy is a decline in the birthrate, which the *Universal Almanac* has predicted will go from seventh place among nations to twentieth by the year 2050. Fewer children may mean a reduced demand for products and will likely decrease the number of jobs for teachers, home builders, electronics manufacturers, and furniture makers. Also, to the embarrassment and frustration of Japanese parents, many young people are rebelling against traditions. According to college professors, those educated outside Japan often hope to learn a second language so they can escape the uncreative Japanese economic market and join more promising ventures in Europe, the Middle East, or the United States.

Because the Japanese system encourages consolidation over small businesses, the managerial elite consists of a few giant conglomerates—Nissan, Mitsubishi, Mitsui, Toyota, and Sumitomo. This, combined with the 60 percent tax placed on the rich in 1992, has resulted in a high concentration of wealth in a tiny percent (.07) of the population.

Housing is also a problem. Japan's concentration of wealth has produced a tightly controlled economy that is centered in Tokyo and around the coastal areas extending northward. Because Japan's urban real estate is expensive, many workers live in suburban or rural settings, where housing and fresh food are cheaper. Workers from outlying areas depend on computer-controlled rail systems and subways, whose daily influx of people overtax cities. To ease the stress of Japan's crowded transportation system, workers live in tiny quarters in cramped urban areas.

At home, apartment dwellers limit themselves to tiny living spaces measured in *tatamis* or the number of straw mats that the floor can accommodate. Consequently, the Japanese home averages 800 square feet, compared with the U.S. average of 1,773 square feet. Cultural historian Michael Wolff notes in *Where We Stand*, "Children's bedrooms, almost always shared by two or more children, tend to be the size of an American walk-in closet. Portable camp stoves are hot sellers each winter, because fewer than 20 percent of Japanese homes have central heating." Although Japan's 60 percent home-ownership

Japanese office workers rest in Tokyo's Brain Mind Gym, an establishment that offers soothing music and light shows within capsulelike headsets. For many Japanese, this program helps to ease the stress and anxiety related to work.

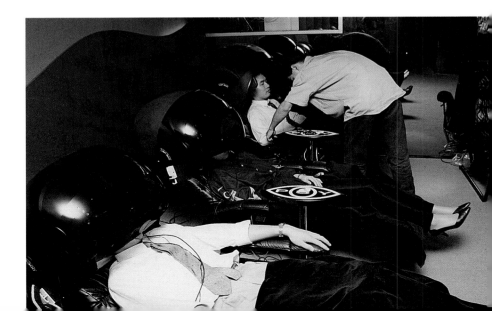

rate tops the U.S. rate by only one percentage point, the contrast in amenities is significant. American journalist James Fallows comments in *Atlantic* magazine, "Anyone who has spent more than a week in Japan understands that its real standard of living is still far below that of Western Europe or the United States." On the average, Japanese homeowners pay nearly triple the cost for residences than Americans so that they can live only half as comfortably.

What little home space is available is increasingly tight in Japan because several generations usually occupy one dwelling. Since religious beliefs require great reverence for the elderly, Japanese families try to give them the best. As reported in *Where We Stand*, "Japanese banks have begun offering multigeneration mortgages that commit children to paying off their parents' debts." At one time, the Japanese, so as not to disturb the unity and order of the family, would not place the aged in nursing homes, as is more customary in the United States. However, as *USA Today* reported in April 1992, the graying of Japan's population has changed this, requiring increased medical care of Japanese senior citizens, who make up a quarter of hospital patients. A shortage of nurses has further upset Japan's plans for secondary-care centers to help relieve the burdens of nursing homes and hospitals.

Finally, Japan's economy is highly sensitive to fluctuations in fuel prices and other commodities because the country depends on imports for most of its energy supply and raw materials for industry.

These and other factors suggest that while Japan and the United States have markedly different economies, both have weaknesses. These weaknesses compel the countries to work together to discover not only where they can establish common ground, but where they must respect one another's differences.

Chapter 4

Different Societies: U.S. Individualism vs. Japanese Unity

F or all their interaction over the past century, the United States and Japan share few social similarities. The United States maintains a society influenced by rugged individualism and a pride for independence that goes back as far as the American Revolution. In addition, at the beginning of the twentieth century, when the United States became a full-fledged nation of immigrants, America's ethnic groups began to assert their own unique cultural identities as a way to be individualistic within the country's "great mosaic."

U.S. Independence and Diversity

American citizens prize freedom of expression on such emotional issues as gun control, abortion, trade unions, and the death penalty. Opinionated citizens express themselves with bumper stickers, lapel buttons, and T-shirts on just about every issue, from animal rights to taxes to pride in their local little league team. Many address issues in common forums, like television talk shows, opinion polls, and letters to the editors of newspapers and magazines.

Along with their openness, their opinions, and their individuality, U.S. citizens value a host of personal freedoms, including the right to privacy and the right to freely

One country boasts a rich mix of cultures, while the other prides itself on its homogeneity.

Opposite:
America's diverse mix of cultures has been called a "great mosaic." Here, individuals from many countries are sworn in as American citizens.

practice their beliefs. The Bill of Rights, the first ten amendments to the U.S. Constitution, guarantees these personal liberties and remains the cornerstone of each American's faith in democracy. The individualistic American spirit also influences the practical way many Americans live. Most commuters prefer to drive to work alone rather than carpool. The noise, air pollution, traffic jams, accidents, and parking problems resulting from the use of so many cars seem to do little to persuade Americans to give up their privacy and self-determinism.

Although individualism and independence are cherished by all Americans, in the large social context they have also created problems. In a nation of diverse ethnic, religious, and economic groups, few government policies or social programs can address the needs of all Americans equally. In many cases, America has paid a price for its rich diversity by creating a system of "special interest groups," in which everyone must speak out for the needs of his or her particular group.

America's emphasis on rugged individualism and free speech is rooted in the Revolution. Here, Revolutionary War heroine Nancy Hart defends her home against the British.

Japanese culture stresses the values of strength through unity, and prosperity through cooperation. Here, workers stretch together before starting their daily routines.

A large percentage of Americans, however, have little or no voice in its government. These Americans are primarily the nation's homeless and poor.

The growth in urban problems of crime, violence, and drug use during the 1970s and 1980s, along with the declining quality in education and growing racial unrest, did much to hamper America's economic and industrial hubs. By 1990, civic officials and police had expended tremendous amounts of energy and used many resources in an effort to stop lawlessness, particularly the sale and distribution of crack cocaine and "designer drugs," which hit the city streets like a plague in the 1980s.

The U.S. health-care system has traditionally been burdened by victims of substance abuse and growing numbers of elderly and poor people who require quality medical care but lack the money or insurance to pay for it.

The Japanese have contained costs by prohibiting doctors from excessive profiteering, but the American Medical Association resists any government interference, particularly fixed rates or other monetary restraints. As a result, U.S. consumers spend 11.5 percent of their incomes on health care, while the Japanese spend only 6.5 percent. Conflicts have raged between U.S. insurance companies and government health agencies as they try to hold down health costs, especially for the poor, the aged, and the increasing numbers of AIDS victims.

Japanese Unity

To understand Japanese society is, in many ways, to understand Japanese business. Because the nation's economy and its method of doing business are so tied to its cultural orientation, it is sometimes hard to separate the success of Japanese business and industry from the apparent "success" of the country's entire way of life. As writer Lance Morrow wrote in *Time* magazine, "Japan is a profoundly communal society organized on almost every level to protect the interests of the Japanese—the welfare of the nation, its business community and its people are one and the same."

The average Japanese workplace is perhaps one of the most obvious examples of Japanese social principles in action. Before the workday begins, adult employees are likely to sing the factory theme song, exercise together, and recite productivity slogans. At breaktime or during meals, many enjoy a camaraderie and a unity of purpose that translate into strong worker loyalty. After work, male co-workers frequently share meetings, dinners, and group recreation. As a group, Japanese workers tend to stress aspects of work and life that tie them together, rather than encourage rebellious or divergent ideas.

To many Americans, the Japanese tendency toward self-submission for the overall good is often viewed as weakness or cowardice. To a people weaned on the

Japanese Students in American Universities: What Are They Learning That We're Not?

Japan sends tens of thousands of students to American schools each year. In 1992, one third of all U.S. MBA candidates were Japanese exchange students. The energetic input of young Japanese entrepreneurs and technicians educated at California Tech, M.I.T., Harvard, Duke, Columbia, and other major U.S. universities provides Japan with a diversity of business approaches it otherwise would lack.

For many, the Japanese focus on business training has called into question America's ways of educating its own young. As Chrysler's Lee Iacocca noted,

"Japan graduates ten engineers for every lawyer, and we graduate ten lawyers for every engineer.... They train people to build a better mousetrap, and we train people to sue the guy with the mousetrap." In addition, foreign-trained students often top American students, producing higher grades and test scores. Less interested in sports, fraternities, and dating, Japanese students easily surpass American classmates by focusing on study and research and often graduating with better records and a firmer grasp of business and economic fundamentals.

concept of rugged individualism, the Japanese may seem lost without the freedoms precious to Americans.

But the Japanese form of unity offers the nation what many see as a unique and sturdy form of freedom; a freedom that has evolved from thousands of years of highly ritualized custom and protocol. Social analyst Steven R. Weisman describes it as "a freedom rooted in security, a low crime rate, and a sense of belonging that seems to have vanished from many societies." The Japanese social system has also prevailed because of the common ethnic makeup of Japanese society, which has allowed such cultural patterns to develop. One saying that captures the Japanese social philosophy appears often in discussions at Japanese conventions: "The nail that sticks up will be hammered down." Consequently, indoctrination into the Japanese philosophy of "group before self" begins in early childhood with exercises that stress sharing and cooperation.

One theory that explains the Japanese craving for unity is the geography of the country. Living in the confines of a small land—an island that isolated itself from outside forces for centuries—the Japanese may feel that unity is the key to survival and the maintenance of peace.

The society-wide emphasis on cooperation and harmony permeates all aspects of Japanese daily life. In the Japanese judicial system, the majority of court cases result in victory for the prosecution. Criminals often apologize instead of appealing to a higher court. Manners, politeness, and respect for elders and authority figures are reinforced on every level and are taught from the earliest stages of childhood. Public and private gardens and flower arrangements typify the Japanese obsession with thrift, balance, and proportion.

In recent times, analysts have disagreed over the dangers of so much single-mindedness in Japan. Some foreign critics, supported by a small group of Japanese, accuse the nation of functioning under the hidden influence of a handful of wealthy, powerful bureaucrats. This oligarchy, or small governing body, is composed of successful corporation owners and politicians who supposedly hold the "keys" to the nation's future.

The Price of Unity

As is true for the United States, Japan's prosperous society has not evolved without a price. In the last quarter of the twentieth century, Japan has also faced growing internal difficulties. Many of their difficulties stem from problems inherent in being a homogeneous society. Although homogeneity has fostered unity and, thus, productivity, it has also bred a tendency for intolerance toward other cultures and peoples. In recent years, this intolerance has fueled some rioting, growing hatreds, and prejudices against Japan's minority populations—most often, Koreans. Social rigidity has also started to concern Japan's youth, who have rebelled with student unrest and protests at Kyoto University.

However, because Japan's social philosophy stresses cooperation and group identity, the Japanese people have a tendency to deemphasize these problems and a host of other problems in favor of maintaining overall social unity.

By sweeping their social problems "under the rug," the Japanese are ignoring serious problems that will only worsen with time. Rather than address those issues, many traditional Japanese prefer to focus on the advantages of the Japanese life-style, which boasts the world's lowest infant mortality rate of five deaths per one thousand live births, and a correspondingly high life expectancy.

In contrast to the U.S. tendency toward individualism, the Japanese stress conformity. From early childhood, Japan's citizens learn to respect thrift, authority, and order. Only 38 percent of Japanese adults use credit cards or voluntarily go into debt, compared with 82 percent of Americans. Less apt to strive for luxury items like fancy cars, furs, and jewelry, the Japanese follow a pattern of regular annual savings averaging $45,118 per household, compared with U.S. savings of $4,201 per family. This tendency toward thrift not only creates a more secure economy by providing its citizens with financial stability, it also fattens the Japanese banking system and increases the nation's investment capabilities.

Complete national unity has its obvious advantages. It allows societal programs to run smoothly and bonds all citizens together with a common purpose. But unity can also hinder a society. For Japan, the emphasis on conformity and submission to authority does not foster the free flow of new or innovative ideas. Because individuals are encouraged to work within the existing system, few question or explore where the system fails or how it can be improved. The effect of this can be seen in many Japanese products. As many people in the automobile and electronics industries have pointed out, there is a certain "sameness" to Japanese products—mostly in their design. Of course, the Japanese would answer that criticism by saying there is also a conformity in the high quality and low price of these items. As with most aspects of production, design, quality, and price must each yield to one another. Is this a negative? That is a matter of debate.

Chapter 5

Uneasy Alliances

Hindered by the differences in their societies, cultural philosophies, life-styles, and economies, Japan and the United States have found it hard to work together. Complicating their efforts was an increasingly bitter trade relationship in the late 1980s and early 1990s. Between 1985 and 1992, U.S. exports to Japan more than doubled, totaling about $50 billion. As a result, Japan felt unfairly pressured to support American industry, and America felt pressured to ease economic downturns by relying more and more on Japanese goodwill.

Negotiations in the spring of 1992 were flawed during an economic summit between Japanese prime minister Kiichi Miyazawa and President George Bush. Bush became ill at a state dinner, collapsed, and had to be helped to a limousine. First Lady Barbara Bush, realizing that her husband was suffering from fatigue and a touch of the flu, had to deliver the president's speech for him in his absence. Americans, watching news reports on television, were acutely aware that this incident was a source of ridicule in Japan, which was fueled by widespread Japanese contempt for American weakness and failure.

However, during the meeting, President Bush's negotiators did help to ease some of the hostility that had heightened between the two nations in previous months.

The two economic superpowers are working hard to understand one another.

Opposite:
A number of strong pro-American campaigns took hold in the United States in 1992, mostly in reaction to rising tensions with Japan.

Although President Bush did make some headway in trade negotiations during his 1992 visit to Japan, many people around the world perceived his trip as a failure. Here, Bush begins his summit with Prime Minister Miyazawa.

They also made more inroads in their mission to control international competition through the use of import tariffs and quotas (protectionism) as opposed to free trade (a free-flowing system based on supply and demand). During the talks, Japanese auto companies promised to double their purchase of American auto parts for a total of $19 billion by 1994. By 1992, the United States was already exporting more goods to Japan than to Italy, Germany, and France combined.

The president made his visit primarily to convince Japan to increase its imports of American-made products. Bush's visit was an effort—for many an all too obvious plea—to help the ailing U.S. economy by bringing the U.S. and Japanese markets into a more acceptable balance.

Despite the president's efforts, U.S. companies still faced a genuine struggle to establish markets in Japan, where prohibitive import taxes and restrictions have kept out American goods. Two examples of American products that have been strictly controlled in Japan are automobiles and rice. For years, U.S. automobile manu-facturers tried to gain a piece of the Japanese-vehicle and agricultural-vehicle markets. The Japanese government, however, defeated these efforts by imposing high import tariffs that raised the price of imported goods beyond competitive levels. Likewise, in order to protect local farmers, Japan's agriculture minister has blocked the wholesale importation of American-grown rice by inflating the price. Although rice produced in the United States is cheaper than Japanese rice, Japan's tariffs make American rice too expensive for Japanese consumers. These trade practices are adhered to by most major economies in the world, and America raises the prices of many Japanese goods for the very same "protectionist" reasons.

A Stormy Relationship

Not all the negative responses to competition occur among Americans. Japan has unleashed anti-American sentiment from its parliament and president. After President Bush's visit to Japan, Yoshio Sakurauchi, the speaker of the lower house of the Diet (Japanese legislative body), called American workers "lazy" and "illiterate." These comments enraged Americans, who were already suffering because of unemployment and feelings of failure in a stubborn recession.

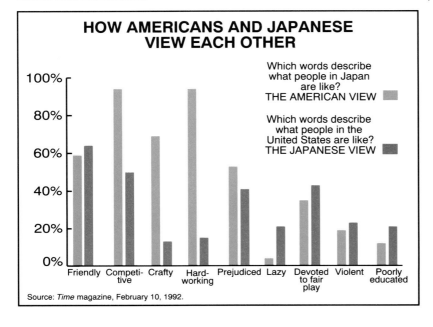

HOW AMERICANS AND JAPANESE VIEW EACH OTHER

Which words describe what people in Japan are like?
THE AMERICAN VIEW

Which words describe what people in the United States are like?
THE JAPANESE VIEW

Source: *Time* magazine, February 10, 1992.

Their frustration and anger started a wave of anti-Japanese protests across the country. Images of Japanese cars being destroyed by angry demonstrators with sledge-hammers filled the evening news. Within days, car dealers and manufacturers were spearheading campaigns to "buy American" as a perfect way to punish Japan *and* help the American economy at the same time. In Warren, Ohio, an ear surgeon, Dr. William Lippy, offered the employees in his clinic $400 cash if they bought a new American car. His program captured the attention of the media and launched his "Jump-Start America" campaign. Within months, he claimed to have 175 firms with 60,000 workers enlisted. Car dealers across the nation posted "Made in America" signs in their showroom windows as auto manufacturers scrambled to produce television commercials that reinforced the same powerful message.

The "Buy American" campaigns appeared to clearly draw the lines between good and bad, "us" versus "them." But the reality of Japan's influence in America was much different. Japanese investment in American business, for example, was already a large part of the American economic landscape. During the week that

Anti-Japanese sentiment spread quickly across the United States in 1992, when a member of the Japanese government called American workers "lazy" and "illiterate." Here an American has paid to bash a Honda.

In the Driver's Seat

In early August 1991, Toyota announced that it was unleashing a new threat to American automakers—the T100 truck, a midsize pickup that competed with the big sellers from Chevrolet and Ford. Headlines in *USA Today, The Wall Street Journal*, and other publications broke the news at a time when American automakers were still reeling from an extended recession that was heavily influenced by declining sales in domestic markets. Previously hurt by the challenge of Japanese cars like Subaru, Mazda, Honda, and Toyota, Detroit worried about Toyota's new model. It could haul three passengers in its cab and full sheets of plywood in its bed. Spokespersons for Detroit noted that both Ford and Chevrolet needed to come up with their own midsize models to keep their hold on this lucrative segment of the American automotive market—one of the few slots left open by the aggressive Japanese.

For American industry—particularly the automotive sector—this scenario is the norm. Since 1950, when America produced nearly 80 percent of the world's automobiles, U.S. auto production has been steadily declining due, in large part, to increased competition from Japan. By 1992, the United States was producing 20.4 percent of the world's autos, behind Japan's 24.2 percent and well behind Europe's 37.7 percent.

A greater disparity existed in the electronics market. Japan produced 43 percent of the world total; Europe, 16 percent; and the United States, 13 percent. The price-to-quality ratio in Japanese products is something even American consumers cannot ignore. In 1989, the Honda Accord became the top-selling car in America.

By the 1990s, Japan also threatened to corner the market on semiconductors and state-of-the-art microchips. Moreover, the Japanese were seriously undercutting American steel production and the dominance of domestic vehicle producers in the United States, notably the three American giants, General Motors (GM), Ford, and Chrysler.

In the few areas where the United States has enjoyed an edge, engineers and marketers must work hard to stay one step ahead of their Japanese competition. It has been a race that is perpetually neck and neck.

Chrysler chairman Lee Iacocca was an outspoken leader in the "Buy American" movement of 1992.

many anti-Japanese protests took place in Louisville, Kentucky, Toyota announced another in a series of $90 million plant expansions. The plant would add two hundred new jobs to the local economy and would provide a sorely needed boost to communities that had been hard-hit by bleak economic times. Total Japanese employment of Americans had risen to 600,000, while Japanese investors held $180 billion in assets (thirty times that of the Germans). Sadahei Kusomoto, chairman and chief executive officer of Minolta's U.S. operations, pointed out in an interview with a *Time* reporter, "It's hard to blame Japan for the recession in the United States.

Japanese tourists visit Rockefeller Center in New York, one of the city's landmarks, which has been sold to Japanese interests.

Ford, GM, and Zenith are moving their plants to Mexico. American companies are giving up manufacturing in this country, while Sony, Toshiba, and Mitsubishi are coming here and opening up major plants."

Many Americans, however, do not see Japanese investment in America as a positive thing. In many sectors of the economy, Japanese investors expanded at a rapid pace. According to *The New York Times*, in the 1980s and early 1990s, Japanese investors took advantage of bankruptcies, low market prices, and the shaky American economy by buying up banks, hotels, industrial parks, construction firms, condominiums, shopping centers, factories, and movie companies. Japanese holding companies now own the Exxon Building in Rockefeller Center, Tiffany's luxury department store, and the ABC Tower in Manhattan; Los Angeles's ARCO Plaza; and most of the hotels on Waikiki Beach. With the high prices of land and development in Japan, Japanese entrepreneurs considered the investments in the United States to be bargains. However, from the U.S. point of view, Japanese investment sounded an alarm that prime segments of the United States may become dominated by foreign interests.

Some suggest that the loss of American capital to foreign investment cannot be blamed totally on Japan's competitiveness. Yet, many Americans have made the island nation a scapegoat, neglecting other nations that are tough business rivals, notably the countries of Western Europe, Hong Kong, Korea, Mexico, India, and Pakistan. All these nations flood the world market with cheap cotton clothing, woolens, electrical appliances, and processed foods.

Bright Spots for America in Japan

Many people have also pointed out that Americans often do not appreciate the many U.S. business successes in Japan, for example, IBM (International Business Machines)

American Industry in Japan

The Japanese consume more than a billion dollars' worth of McDonald's food each year.

The names *Sony*, *Toyota*, and *Honda* can be seen almost everywhere in the American landscape. But how many Japanese movie stars or television programs are "household names" for the average American? And how many Americans eat sushi on a regular basis? The answer to both these questions is "not too many." In Japan, however, American culture is everywhere; it is an essential part of growing up "hip" in Japan.

What are the "hippest" clothes for Japanese youth living in Tokyo, Osaka, and Yokohama? Baggy chinos, a sweatshirt from Stanford University, a pair of Bass Weejuns shoes, and a Washington Redskins hat. And are these hip Japanese wearing their clothes to sushi bars? Not at all. They're munching on Cool Ranch Doritos, all-beef franks from the Chicago Dog restaurant, or pizza ordered from Chicago Pizza. All together, the Japanese consume more than a billion dollars' worth of McDonald's fast food each year and another billion in soft drinks made by the Coca-Cola Company. After dinner at the golden arches, it's off to the movies, where the blockbuster charts look almost exactly like those in America. For the really big winners, like T*erminator 2*, *Home Alone*, and *Pretty Woman*, tickets must be purchased days in advance. A recent M.C. Hammer concert sold out all 56,000 seats within hours of the box-office opening. Both the Super Bowl and the World Series are broadcast live in Japan.

Many Japanese are not content to experience America in bits and pieces in their city shops and movie theaters. And those who travel to the States for a firsthand look make up an enormous tourist industry that began a major boom in the late 1980s. More than 3 million Japanese visited America in 1991, spending a total of $10 billion. Almost 1.5 million Japanese traveled to Hawaii, including 20 percent of all Japanese honeymooners. After the hit series "Twin Peaks" aired in Japan, travel agents in Snoqualmie, Washington—where the series was filmed—started selling trips and tours that went as high as $1,600 for a five-day outing.

Mickey and Minnie Mouse wear kimonos at Tokyo's Disneyland.

and Apple computers, Kodak film and cameras, Kellogg's cereals, Coca-Cola, Elizabeth Arden cosmetics, Schick shaving products, and Heinz foods. Other thriving American interests in Japan include Hollywood movies and television series, computer software, and fast-food chains.

America has also outperformed Japan in creating jobs in its own country, producing 4 percent more new jobs annually than its rival. Moreover, the United States manages to feed itself and much of the world while using only 2.9 percent of its working population, compared with 7.6 percent of Japanese citizens working in agriculture.

Japan in America

A growing trend to combine forces in manufacturing firms has resulted in American managers and workers running U.S.-based Japanese factories in the automobile and construction industries. Japanese manufacturers have begun setting up operations in the United States in much the same way that Sharp Electronics in Memphis, Tennessee, has done. There, local workers assemble parts under the supervision of Japanese-trained American bosses. Other experiments in international business include Fujitsu's computer-disk plant in Portland, Oregon; a Nissan auto plant in Smyrna, Tennessee; a Mazda factory in Flat Rock, Michigan; General Motor's alliance with Toyota in Fremont, California; and a plant built by Mitsubishi in Bloomington, Illinois. Throughout the United States, company names like Hitachi, Daiwa, Mitsui, Sumitomo, Honda, and Kajima are printed on employee time cards and paychecks almost as much as names like General Mills, Sears Roebuck, and Texaco.

Learning from Each Other

Cooperative efforts between the two nations had a significant role in improving U.S. attitudes toward productivity.

As the United States struggled to cut its losses in the world economy, it took a closer look at Japan's philosophy and business practices. American business leaders envied those elements of Japan's style that could be adapted to America's free-market system.

By 1992, a number of examples of new American business successes began to get coverage in national magazines and economic journals. Many U.S. companies, like GM's Saturn Corporation, Andersen Windows, Microsoft Corporation, and the Timberland boot company, built their success primarily on the principles of quality and loyalty, two elements that are integral to the Japanese corporate system. General Motors found that its investment in its Saturn cars, which were designed specifically to compete with Japanese automobiles, paid off more quickly than expected. The Saturn plant in Spring Hill, Tennessee, relies on the teamwork of employees to keep costs down. Andersen Windows and

Saturn Corporation, owned by General Motors, was one of America's automobile success stories in the early 1990s.

Japanese astronaut Mamoru Mohri was part of a NASA team that flew on a U.S. Space Shuttle mission in September 1992.

Timberland, which produces waterproof work boots, both emphasize quality in their products and do extensive testing. Microsoft succeeded in gaining a large share of the computer software market by emphasizing the customer's needs in developing its new programs.

The success of cooperative efforts with Japan is growing, too. Companies like Philip Morris have gained access to Japanese television advertising, greatly boosting the sale of American cigarettes and at the same time profiting the Japanese media. A more powerful example illustrates cooperation in the highly competitive computer industry. In July 1992, *U.S. News and World Report* praised the joint venture of Advanced Micro Devices with Japan's Fujitsu Ltd. to build a $700 million factory to produce flash memory chips. As the result of a major breakthrough in design, these unique computer chips exceed the many capabilities of current models by maintaining stored information even if the flow of electricity is halted.

At the same time, Japanese managers who had to adapt to work in U.S. manufacturing had to deal with America's more aggressive trade unions and accommodate people of both sexes and all races in work environments that—unlike many in Japan— could not discriminate on the basis of sex or race.

As Americans wrestled with the serious economic woes of the early 1990s—a huge deficit, unemployment, bank failures, and a nagging recession—business professionals became more open to arriving at an understanding with their rivals. Many learned the Japanese language, while launching fact-finding missions in Japan. There they toured factories, studied research and development methods, and examined managerial techniques. Others openly welcomed Japanese tourism, which bolstered the economy and helped ease unemployment, particularly in large cities. Generally speaking, the relaxing of fear and suspicion between America and Japan benefited both nations by increasing cooperative efforts.

In a joint venture in September 1992, American and Japanese citizens worked together on a space shuttle mission, which was dubbed "Spacelab-J." The NASA (National Aeronautics and Space Administration) space shuttle Endeavor had a Japanese astronaut, Mamoru Mohri, among the seven crew members aboard for the eight-day mission that began September 12. Mohri, Japan's first professional astronaut, worked with American astronauts on many Japanese experiments, which included the incubation of fish and chicken eggs, space motion sickness, and the delivery of intravenous fluids in weightlessness. During the mission, information from space was sent back to Japanese scientists working alongside American scientists at the Kennedy Space Center in Florida. Japan also helped to pay for the joint space mission.

If such ventures are indications of what is to come in Japanese-American relations, perhaps the future will be brighter for both countries and for the world.

Chapter 6

The Future of the Global Economy

During the 1992 presidential primaries, Massachusetts senator Paul Tsongas sounded what became a familiar refrain among economists: "The Cold War is over, and Japan won."

Although the statement was intended to be primarily ironic, it effectively pointed out one of the greatest economic challenges facing the United States for the future. Tsongas was trying to point out that, after the Cold War ended, America's economy needed to be drastically reoriented. Much of the rationale for America's role as the "global watchdog" for democracy vanished with the collapse of the Soviet Union, and with it went much of the need to fuel America's giant military and defense industry.

While the end of the Cold War made most Americans feel safer and more secure, it also presented the nation with the difficult challenge of converting much of its military-based industry into other means of production. Because military-related industry played such a large part in the overall makeup of America's Cold War economy,

Cooperation between the economic superpowers will be the key to survival.

Opposite:
Both Japan and America will face new challenges in manufacturing for the twenty-first century.

many think that the transition to other industries will be complicated and time-consuming. It will most likely involve targeting new areas for technological and industrial development and, ironically, it will most likely rely partly on Japanese investment to make those new areas work. In 1992, president-elect Bill Clinton pledged to make the nation's transition to a non–Cold War economy one of the top priorities of his administration.

Japan, too, has many complex economic challenges to overcome in the future. As its industrial base grows, it must find more and more outlets to sell Japanese goods. Because of its small size, Japan will always be limited in the number of goods it can purchase from other nations and will most likely never have the "buying clout" of larger blocs, such as the European Community or the United States. As a mountainous island nation, Japan will always have limited space and, thus, limited agricultural resources. These limitations will create an increasing reliance on other nations for food and raw materials that Japan does not have. That is a vulnerability Japan must constantly protect.

Similar Paths

Perhaps more than either of the two nations is likely to acknowledge, the United States and Japan share a similar future. In a report for Washington periodical *Foreign Affairs*, former U.S. ambassador to Japan Mike Mansfield noted that, "The most important bilateral [two-way] relationship in the world today is that between the United States and Japan. . . . The victor and vanquished of World War II have become the cornerstones of the international economic system, together producing almost 40 percent of the world's GNP (gross national product)." As a pair, the two countries form the power base of the Pacific, strengthening weaker nations with prestige and economic support. Both world powers, unwilling to concede any

Russian youths wave their flags in a show of newfound independence. By 1991, the end of communism in the Soviet Union and in most of Eastern Europe created a vast but untapped new free market.

leadership to other nations, are determined to keep growing economically. Likewise, fear of foreigners and strong nationalism sometimes influence thinking in both U.S. and Japanese cultures and can challenge progress.

Still, Japan and the United States face many of the same challenges in the global economy. Both countries, for instance, face increased competition from outside sources that include:

- a growing competitiveness from Mexico, Canada, Korea, Singapore, and Taiwan
- developing third-world economies that are playing an increasingly significant role in the cheap production of manufactured goods
- the increasing productivity of Germany, which has been labeled an economic miracle
- the collapse of Soviet communism, which has created great potential for new free markets
- the resurgence of Eastern Europe as a democratic stronghold and the formation of a powerful economic union in the European Community.

Both the United States and Japan have also faced the prospect of coping with the busts following the "booms" in the stock market. Japan's seemingly endless supply of ready cash bottomed out in the spring of 1992. In addition, scandals lessened consumer confidence, tax revenues dropped, and Americans showed less interest in buying Japanese goods. According to *USA Today*, in August 1992, the Nikkei—Japan's stock market—suffered a 36 percent fall, greatly outdistancing even the worst U.S. troubles on Wall Street.

In America, trouble brewed in many financial areas, especially in the banking industry. By 1992, Citicorp, once the most profitable bank in the world, ranked twenty-third. Even more troubling was the fact that Citicorp remained the only American bank in the top forty-five worldwide.

Both Japan and the United States, faced with an aging work force, must rise to the challenge of restaffing factories and offices in the future with their brightest and most creative young talents. For Japan, this may mean opening more doors to female employees and to the 750,000 Koreans who make up 0.6 percent of the population.

For the United States, this involves improving education and technology training for all workers and finding ways to utilize the talents of people in all segments of society, including America's previously unskilled workers. To spread the American dream to all segments of the population, local governments in the future need to turn to a broader, more effective educational system that can challenge and motivate America's rich mix of students.

In Japan, where strict education has been a top priority for generations, the challenge will be offering students broader perspectives on other cultures. These views will give them the understanding they need to work within a global community. For both Japan and the United States, these matters require a thorough rethinking of educational and social priorities.

In the final analysis, both Japan and the United States must realize their interdependence and their roles as the leaders of the global economy. At the same time, these two nations must remember that the well-being of the world economy depends not only on the front-runners but also on the smaller but extremely important contributions of other nations. World economic health depends on German and Korean technology, Mideastern and Mexican oil, French and English drug research, and even on the successful sharing of scientific and technological information with scientists and researchers from the former Soviet Union. As the European Community increases its organization and influence, it will continue to become an even more significant factor in world trade. Japan and the United States must react and adapt their strategies if they are to compete with the European Community trading bloc, now the largest in the world. In 1992 and early 1993, the United States stood poised to begin its journey toward greater economic competitiveness. The new

Former General Motors chairman Robert Stempel (left) met with Nissan Motor Company president Yutaka Kume in May 1992 to discuss cooperative efforts between America and Japan in the automobile industry.

Clinton adminstration planned to implement a number of programs that were aimed at learning from foreign countries as America adapted its economic strategies to the new global marketplace.

The Challenge of Cooperation

As with many things, one of the most accurate ways to chart a course for the future is to learn from the past. After World War II, American and Japanese cooperation turned a small, devastated island nation into one of the most successful economies in the world. This success, however, was achieved only by an openness and a willingness to put petty cultural differences aside for the good of the ultimate goal.

Many political analysts agree that, if Japan and the United States want to remain strong in the twenty-first century, they must begin again to cooperate and learn

The Japanese food chain Sushi Boy began selling in U.S. markets in October 1992. As America and Japan learn more about each other, they will be better able to share the riches of their cultures.

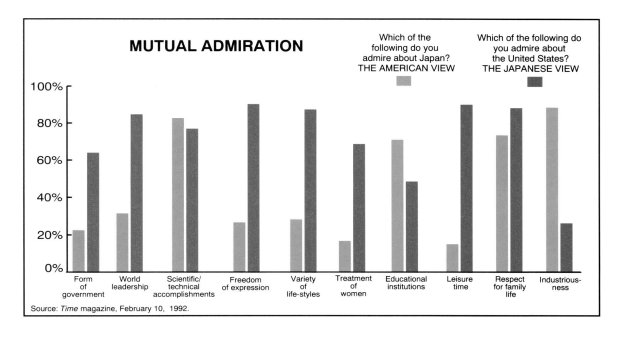

MUTUAL ADMIRATION

Which of the following do you admire about Japan? THE AMERICAN VIEW

Which of the following do you admire about the United States? THE JAPANESE VIEW

Form of government · World leadership · Scientific/technical accomplishments · Freedom of expression · Variety of life-styles · Treatment of women · Educational institutions · Leisure time · Respect for family life · Industriousness

Source: *Time* magazine, February 10, 1992.

from each other. Although there are pitfalls inherent in the societal and business approaches of both nations, there is much valuable knowledge to be gained from their successes.

Many prejudices and perceptions must be changed in order for both countries to work toward progress. American businesspeople must dispense with any attitudes that American culture is somehow superior to all others. In addition, they must cultivate a greater willingness to learn about the Japanese. As Texas investor Richard Fisher said in a 1992 *Time* magazine interview, "When I grew up, we were the sole proprietors of the world's economic system. Now we're being asked to be one of the partners. But we still don't have any collective knowledge of Japan; none of our political leaders speak Japanese. We are dealing from a vantage point of weakness. We need to clean up our own act first, and then deal with them on a basis of mutual respect."

American businesspeople have resisted more intimate contact with the Japanese for other reasons as well. Many accuse the Japanese of being extremely picky about products as a means of limiting imports. They also criticize a perceived overattention to external detail and an overemphasis on hierarchy and teamwork. They frown upon what they see as a stifling "one job for life" mentality. Whatever merits these criticisms may have, they tend to mask Japanese characteristics that have proved to be very successful in the world of business.

Japanese businesspeople are not at all reluctant to criticize Americans. Many of them say that American companies demonstrate numerous weaknesses, including a heavy-handedness and an arrogance in the board room, too high a ratio of overpaid white-collar workers to laborers, an inability to inspire worker responsibility and company loyalty, a lack of concern for research and development, and bloated budgets—which provide executives with 3,500 private jets vs. Japan's 18.

It is perhaps unrealistic to believe that all of these mutual criticisms and differences can be erased in the future. In the broadest sense, the two cultures have evolved from such different roots that they will most likely never be able to truly accommodate one another on many levels. But both nations share an overriding dedication to remain at the top of the world's economic ladder, and it is on the playing field of global economic competition that these two players will meet. Though they will always remain rivals, the two countries will most likely realize that much can be learned by observing the successes of competitors and by working together with economic allies toward common goals.

Chronology

1853	Commodore Matthew C. Perry establishes commercial relations with Japan.
1895	Japan defeats China as part of its expansion policy.
1899	Henry Ford organizes the Detroit Automobile Company, whose assembly-line concept was adapted by Japan after World War II.
1905	Japan defeats Russia as part of its expansion policy.
December 7, 1941	Japan attacks Pearl Harbor, Hawaii.
December 8, 1941	Amercia declares war on Japan and its allies.
1942	President Franklin Roosevelt orders U.S citizens of Japanese parentage to internment camps.
August 6, 1945	The United States drops an atomic bomb on the Japanese city of Hiroshima.
August 9, 1945	The United States bombs the Japanese city of Nagasaki.
September 2, 1945	Japan officially surrenders to the United States. U.S. occupation of Japan, which had begun in August, continues.
April 28, 1952	The Allied occupation of Japan, which helped to educate Japan in Western business and manufacturing methods, ends.
1956	Japan joins the United Nations.
1964	Japan becomes the first Asian nation to host the Olympics.
1972	America's postwar control of Japan officially ends, with the return of Okinawa and other Japanese islands.
1973	An oil embargo causes prices to skyrocket creating shortages around the world and deflating U.S. economic supremacy.
1980s	Japan invests heavily in U.S. real estate and makes its presence felt in large corporations.
Early 1990s	U.S. exports to Japan reach an unprecedented high as the American economy lags. The United States develops the highly successful Saturn automobile to compete with Japanese cars. Concerned about Japan's economic inroads in the United States, Americans launch a "Buy American" campaign.

Early 1990s, con't.

Japan threatens to surpass the United States and become the world's number one economic power. George Bush visits Japan in the spring of 1992 for an economic summit. The United States signs a trade pact with Canada and Mexico in August 1992 to remedy its trade imbalance.

Early 1990s, con't.

Japan's economy begins to show signs of weakness. As a result, the United States and Japan undertake joint economic ventures. In July 1992, the two countries cooperate to build a factory to produce flash memory chips. On September 12, 1992, they launch a space-shuttle mission, "Spacelab-J."

For Further Reading

Bolitho, Harold. *Jeiji Japan*. Minneapolis, MN: Lerner Publications, 1980.

Chant, Christopher. *World War II: The Pacific War*. North Bellmore, NY: Marshall Cavendish, 1992.

Davidson, Judith. *Japan: Where East Meets West*. Discovering Our Heritage Series. Minneapolis, MN: Dillon Press, 1983.

Dolan, Edward F. *America in World War II: 1943*. Brookfield, CT: Millbrook Press, 1992.

Greene, Carol. *Japan*. Chicago IL: Childrens Press, 1983.

Schlesinger, Arthur M., Jr., ed. *Harry S. Truman*. Broomall, PA: Chelsea House, 1990.

Smith, Nigel. *The United States Since 1945*. New York: Franklin Watts, 1990.

Zurlo, Tony. *Japan: Superpower of the Pacific*. New York: Dillon Press, 1991.

Index

Acknowledgments and photo credits

Cover: Blackbirch Graphics, Inc.; p.4: Wide World Photos; p.8: ©Terry Arthur/
Gamma-Liaison; p.10: Wide World Photos; p.14: Associated Press/Wide World
Photos; p.15: Associated Press/Wide World Photos; p.16: Associated Press/Wide
World Photos; p. 17: Associated Press/Wide World Photos; p.18: ©Blackbirch
Graphics Inc.; p. 20: ©Frank Fisher/Gamma-Liaison; p.22: ©Ken Hammond/
Department of Defense; p. 24: Wide World Photos; p.25: ©Bryce Lankard/
Gamma-Liaison; p.30: Wide World Photos; p.32: ©Greenwood/Gamma-
Liaison; p.34: ©Blackbirch Graphics; p.35: Wide World Photos; p.40: ©Michael
J. Okoniewski/Gamma-Liaison; p.42: Wide World Photos; p.44: Associated
Press/Wide World Photos; p.45: Wide World Photos; p.46: Wide World Photos;
p.47: ©Jim Bryant/Gamma-Liaison; p.47: Wide World Photos; p.49: Wide
World Photos; p.50: National Aeronautics and Space Administration; p.52:
©Kathleen Campbell/Gamma-Liaison; p.55: Wide World Photos; p.57: Wide
World Photos; p.58: ©Kaku Kutita/Gamma-Liaison.
Maps and Graphs by Sandra Burr.